Endorsements

"Far too often, the families of incarcerated individuals are the forgotten victims of crime. They have few resources to help them navigate the complexities of the criminal justice system or to guide them within the confusing maze of their emotions. Lennie Spitale has provided a tremendous tool that meets this need. Written from the crucible of his own experiences, both as a former felon and as a veteran jail/prison minister, **Lennie offers clear direction and sensitive advice** *for the reader. This booklet should be read by everyone who is experiencing the trauma of having a family member incarcerated."*

—**Dr. W. Thomas Beckner**, assistant vice president
of national ministry, Good News Jail & Prison Ministry

"I wish I had known of a resource like this when my son was arrested. This booklet is filled with **valuable information that will help you understand the legal process** *when your loved one is jailed. If you are looking for emotional, technical and spiritual support, this is the resource you need."*

—**Carol Kent**, speaker and author,
When I Lay My Isaac Down

"Help! My Loved One Is in Jail. What Do I Do Now?"

By Lennie Spitale

The IPM Library

Over two million people are incarcerated in the United States today. Countless more family and friends must cope with these difficult situations. The "IPM Library," a new booklet series of the Institute for Prison Ministries at the Billy Graham Center, was designed to assist family and friends by providing a road map that will systematically highlight the emotional, social, relational, financial and spiritual struggles which come with having a loved one incarcerated. Each booklet will include a situation-appropriate, evangelistic message.

Acknowledgements

To Karen Swanson, director of the Institute for Prison Ministries at the Billy Graham Center at Wheaton College, whose partnership, initiation, ideas, energy and suggestions for the project kept it on course.

To my wife, Gwen, whose love for the Lord and desire to serve Him is a constant encouragement to me. Her faith in our great God continues to grow and is demonstrated by a determination to shed worldly pursuits and to fill her thoughts and purposes for His kingdom.

To prison ministry people, whose tireless efforts to bring Christ's compassion behind bars have provided me with many examples.

To the prisoners and their families, who suffer separation and personal pain, and are the very people for whom this has been written. May each of you find the true comfort that is found only in Jesus Christ and through faith in Him.

To God, the source of all comfort, "who comforts us in all our troubles so that we can comfort others with the same comfort we ourselves have received from Him" (2 Corinthians 1:3-4).

*"Help! My Loved One Is in Jail.
What Do I Do Now?"*
By Lennie Spitale

Copyright © 2007. Pubished by Evangelism and
Missions Information Service (EMIS), a division
of the Billy Graham Center at Wheaton College.

EMIS
P.O. Box 794
Wheaton, IL 60189
Phone: 630.752.7158
Email: emis@wheaton.edu
Website: www.billygrahamcenter.org/emis

ISBN 978-1-879089-41-9

CONTENTS

INTRODUCTION 9

CHAPTER ONE
Receiving the News 11

CHAPTER TWO
To Bail or Not to Bail?. 21

CHAPTER THREE
Communicating with Your Loved One 37

CHAPTER FOUR
The Legal Process 45

CHAPTER FIVE
Hiring an Attorney. 51

CHAPTER SIX
God's Plan for You 59

INTRODUCTION

You are holding this in your hands because someone you know has just been arrested. It feels like you are living in a nightmare. "This can't be happening," you keep repeating to yourself. "How did this happen?" "What do I do now?" "How do I help him[1]?" "How do I get him out of there?" "*Should* I get him out of there?" "With whom do I speak to fix this?"

If these and similar questions are racing around in your head, then read on. This booklet was designed to help you work through this unfamiliar process. Although the suggestions mentioned here are primarily intended for those who have never before experienced the sudden incarceration of a loved one, they should also prove to be helpful (at least by way of reminder) to those who have been through it before. It can serve as a checklist for process points you may need to consider.

The emotions that seek to overwhelm you (although unpreventable) can hinder you from taking the most thoughtful steps. You may be unfamiliar with this process and feel inadequate in

---

1. Although we understand that both men and women are incarcerated, for ease of reading we have chosen to use the pronoun "he" where we talk about your loved one who has been arrested.

terms of making the right decisions. Additionally, a specific course of action that might be right for one situation may not be right for another. This booklet is designed to give you the pieces you need so that you can thoughtfully arrive at your own course of action.

Our hearts go out to you and we want you to know that we have asked God to grant you the peace that only He can give you. As Jesus calmed the stormy seas simply by speaking to them,[2] our prayer is that He will bring a measure of calmness into the "storm" that you are now experiencing.

---

2. Luke 8:22-25

CHAPTER ONE

Receiving the News

It may be just a few days, or even a few hours, since you first heard that your loved one was arrested. You *heard* the news, but it seemed like it came to you as part of a bad dream. This can't be true, you told yourself. But the rational side of you knew that it was. The days since you first heard the news have been a nightmare. It feels like your whole world has been overturned. The former activities with which you had been filling your days suddenly seem so trivial and unimportant. You find yourself thinking and worrying about your loved one all the time.

It probably started with a phone call: "Mom, Dad, I'm in jail." Perhaps it was your spouse, a relative or a friend who told you the news. It may have been a girlfriend or boyfriend. It may have been a police officer. Perhaps you first heard about it on the news or in the local newspaper. However you heard the report, it still came as a shock. You may not have thought about it in those terms (and you might not even have been all that surprised), but the first thing you must accept is that you have not had time to thoroughly digest what it may mean.

Do not make a rash decision; you need time to process the situation as realistically as possible. In spite of your loved one's situation, the first person you must tend to is you. You, and the others who are closely related to the person in jail. All of you will not be much help to him if you start making decisions in a panic mode. Some of the very first steps (or non-steps) that people make at the outset can often have a bearing on future events.

First, realize that your immediate response is an emotional one. You are afraid. Your adrenalin is running high and your mind is racing through one fearful scenario after another. And all of them are bad. You could be anywhere on the emotional spectrum, depending on your own unique response system. You may find yourself immediately praying or pleading with God for help. Or you may be angry with God. "How could you let this happen, God?" you cry. Or you may have no thoughts about Him at all.

Fear is the most common emotion experienced. Every dragon that could be lurking in the recesses of possibility suddenly becomes, for you, a probability. You immediately think about all the bad things you have heard happen in prison. You wonder how your loved one is handling it and what awful scenario he might be facing. What if someone beats him up? Or worse!

All you know is that you need to contact your loved one. But you also need perspective. Do bad things happen in jail? Yes, they do. Nothing is a guarantee. But first, stop and consider the facts: most of those bad things do not happen to the majority of people who wind up in jail. We are not trying to falsely encourage you, nor are we trying to frighten you. But what you need most right now is perspective. Fear has a way of making the terrible dragon called "What-if" seem like his name is "Definitely-will." That is the nature of fear. But when we slow down and take a realistic look at this fire-breathing dragon, we may discover that his true size is really quite smaller than we had first imagined. Try hard not to live in the land of "what-if"; instead, try to deal with "what-is." The reality is discouraging enough without stringing yourself out in an unmerciful panic mode.

We readily acknowledge that this is much more easily said than done. Do not feel like a failure if you cannot keep yourself from over-worrying. A certain level of it is completely normal in this context. However, being driven crazy by an unrealized fear will be physically harmful to you. It will also interfere with making good decisions.

In this wild soup of emotions, you will also experience a few other ingredients. In addition to the initial shock and fear, it is likely you are also experiencing a measure of anger. (You may already have apologized to someone for lashing out at him or her shortly after receiving the news.) You are not alone in this. Fear and anger are very common responses to many who have been in your situation. But it helps to try and understand where that anger is coming from. Here are some likely suspects:

1. Helplessness. You have come face to face

with the fact that you cannot immediately rush in and save your loved one out of his situation. The frustration you are experiencing at not being able to rescue him causes you to feel totally helpless. This frustration can lead to anger, which may be specifically directed at someone or something indirectly connected to the situation. You are only using convenient targets at which you can vent your frustration. The real problem is that you feel helpless.

Another target of your anger can be directed at someone or something you perceive to be the *reason* your loved one is in jail. You may blame *them* for what has happened and convince yourself that it was *their* influence that got your loved one into trouble. This might be true, or it might also reveal a pattern of enablement that continues to make excuses for your loved one's actions. (We will speak more on this later.)

The important thing for you to consider right now, however, is that if your attack is directed at someone who should be a part of the helping team (such as a spouse or other family member), you will only succeed in weakening the help your loved one should receive. If you know that you have already lashed out at someone in this way, go to the person and ask for his or her forgiveness. You *need* each other.

Your anger could also be directed at yourself. "If only I had done such and such," you say to yourself. You think that the fact that your loved one is sitting in jail means that you have somehow been a failure. Only you can ultimately answer that question, but you should assess it accurately. If your current lifestyle has contributed to a criminal decision your loved one has made, then you need to identify where (and how) that is true. But if you have tried your best to instill a measure of right and wrong in the person's life, then remember that your loved one made a choice to go in a different direction. As much as we would like to remove the repercussions of that choice, none of us are immune to the law of consequences.

A final person you may be angry at is the offender himself. Sometimes we do not like to admit this because it is a time of great worry and concern for your loved one. We do not like to think that we are adding to his misery by being mad at him. But the fact that your family is now in disarray because of your loved one's actions makes you mad. Your family is experiencing guilt and embarrassment because of the person sitting in jail. Personal schedules must be changed, court appearances must be made and money you were not expecting to spend may now need to be redirected. To deny that you may be angry at your incarcerated loved one will not be helpful when trying to make sound decisions in the days ahead.

2. Shame and embarrassment. Although you are not the one charged with the crime, it is common for some people to experience feelings of shame or guilt in connection with the events. Personal names may now appear in the paper; and sometimes, depending on the nature of the crime, you and your family can experience great embarrassment regarding the specific details of the charges. And although these feelings may be necessarily pushed to a backburner as you try to deal with your immediate fears, they can slowly gain strength as the days go by. During the first phone call, both you and your loved one may have been in tears as you spoke; however, after a few days the reality that more and more "others" are learning about your ordeal lurks as an uncomfortable stranger in the back of your mind. If children are involved, do not be surprised to learn that unsympathetic peers who have learned about the arrest may be teasing them at school. This is when we discover on a deeper level that the consequences of one person's actions affect the lives of more than just the offender. When one person is arrested for a crime, others will suffer as well. As you consider which steps to take for the person in jail, pause briefly to consider who else may be suffering as a result. Think about what you can do to acknowledge or alleviate his or her pain.

Remember that emotions do not concern thinking; they concern feeling. Some people (and this is sometimes more true for fathers) deal with their emotional responses by shutting them down. They can go into a mode of denial. Such behavior may have the appearance of being in control and able to make sound decisions, but in reality, it may also be a self-defense mode. We all need a safe place to express our feelings. Don't go it alone. Do not withdraw.

Steps to Dealing with the Initial Shock

Here are some suggested steps that can help to make this initial phase of shock more tolerable.

1. Slow down and reach out. Resist the driving, relentless urge to "fix it." Slow yourself down and get good help. You are not alone in this experience. It has happened to millions of others. Sometimes we think that this awful thing has never happened to anybody else. Intellectually, we know this is ridiculous, but we can find ourselves thinking that we alone have been singled out for this incredible bit of bad news. We may feel embarrassed and ashamed. While we know that other people have their share of serious problems (whether physical, marital or financial), we tend to think that we are the only ones in our social circle who now have a criminal in the family.

2. Talk to someone. If you are married, talk first to your spouse. Be kind to each other. The sudden incarceration of a child has driven many wedges between married couples. The reasons are many, but it usually centers on disagreement as to what responses you are now required to make. Try hard to understand each other's viewpoint. You must both be willing to listen to the other's concerns and be willing to compromise. Again, let me remind you to not be driven entirely by your emotional response. That is why we need help in sorting this out.

But whether you are married or not, seek outside, mature counsel. If this is true for married couples, it becomes essential for a single parent.

Perhaps you have a trusted friend whose wisdom and outlook you respect. You may know someone who has experience with the criminal justice system. You might have a support group with whom you can openly share your feelings. Perhaps there is a pastor or counselor you could meet with. Whatever you do, do not go it alone. Since you are likely to be experiencing intense emotions, you need someone who is wise and caring, but less emotionally involved.

Many people have chosen to isolate themselves from other people, or to pull back from the social settings of their normal routines. This, too, is common—and you must resist it. Because a sense of shame, guilt or embarrassment may be present, we try to protect ourselves from hurt by withdrawing from people we feel "will talk" or be quick to judge. Try to keep in mind that your loved one's choice was not yours; it was his. (Your loved one may, in fact, be feeling very badly about the pain he has caused you. If he thought that you were losing friends over this, he could feel even worse.) You may experience insensitive responses; some people are just like that. But your true friends want to help you; do not hide from them.

The incarceration of your loved one will bring new changes to your routine; this is inevitable. You will be facing serious choices and going places that were formerly alien to you. But try hard to not drastically change the "normal" routine of your life by withdrawing from those activities that best provide you with social support. This includes meeting with friends, going to the gym or to social events, attending support groups or going to church. Make an attempt to keep these connections alive as much as possible. In spite of how you feel now, they will be an encouragement to you when you need them most. In addition to seeking balance, wisdom and perspective, we all need to know we are loved and supported.

While seeking counsel from others, do not make their advice a one-time event. Continue to involve them in your decisions. Seek out a few, special people who will commit to walking with you throughout this process.

3. Seek out counselors, not clones. We all have a tendency to seek out those people whom we know will most agree with us. This is especially true if we tend to be strong-willed individuals and are convinced that we alone know the best approach to take with our loved one in jail. However, what we need most is someone who is committed enough to our well-being that he or she will tell us things we may not want to hear. If we look for those who will only agree with our predisposed opinions, then we are merely talking to ourselves. We have succeeded in finding a clone, not a true counselor.

CHAPTER TWO

To Bail or Not to Bail?

This is one of the toughest decisions you will have to make. At first glance, you might think it is a no-brainer—of course you should bail him out! But there are some significant reasons why the opposite choice may, in some cases, be the better option. Here are some factors you should consider.

1. Financial restrictions and job endangerment. For some, bail is not an option simply because it cannot be afforded. If the charges are fairly serious, and the bail is high, you may have to weigh the cost of bail against attorney fees. If the person in jail was also a contributor to the family financial picture, then that money will no longer be coming in. If there are children in the relationship, daycare expenses may now have to be considered if the remaining spouse has to find additional work. Adding to the financial burden, phone calls from the correctional facility are usually higher than normal rates. In some cases, exorbitantly so.

Choosing to not bail someone out can affect not only the financial situation of the family, but may also impact whether or not the accused will be able to keep his job. Some defendants choose to not tell their employers that they are facing legal entanglements. This is understandable; why lose one's employment for an outcome that may yet be questionable? However, be prepared for the likelihood that the offense has already been published in the local papers. Even if bailed out, subsequent court appearances will require the defendant to take time off from work. These repeated absences are difficult to hide.

If the defendant's employer knows the details of the arrest, the particular nature of the crime may pose a perceived threat to the company's reputation. In such cases, an employer may choose to terminate the employee. If this happens (and only if you want to challenge the firing), check with your loved one's lawyer as to the legality of the employer's decision. In most cases, however, be prepared to accept the employer's actions in the end. This is based on two reasons. First, employers can find their own reasons to legally dismiss someone they do not want to keep. Second, even if the lawyer succeeded in keeping your loved one employed, the "victory" will probably make the atmosphere at work extremely uncomfortable. However, discuss the options with the lawyer, especially if loss of a significant amount of accrued benefits is also in play.

2. Pre-arrest lifestyle. This is one of the most significant factors you should consider when deciding on the question of bail. What was the lifestyle pattern of the accused just prior to arrest? What was he doing? Was he living a responsible life or was he in a constant state of rebellion and negative activity? If the person was still living at home, was he living in obedience to his parents or was he defiant and unresponsive to discipline? Was he breaking curfews and out at all hours? Were there times when he didn't even come home at night?

If the answer to any of these questions is on the negative side, then you may want to think twice before you bail the person out too soon. It is a basic principle of life that actions bear consequences; and an arrest is a consequence to a negative action. If the arrested individual was previously unwilling to change repeatedly negative behavior, then one of the strongest deterrents to such behavior is to experience the inevitably harsh consequences.

Only you can assess whether or not the consequence warrants the offense, but sometimes it is helpful to step back and look at the larger picture. An isolated action may or may not warrant a prolonged stretch in a jail cell, but if this consequence is the cumulative result of a generally irresponsible lifestyle, then bailing the person out too soon will not force him to see the cause and effect of his actions. It could, in fact, reinforce that negative lifestyle by further enabling it.

Consequences are good for personal development; removing them too soon removes their intended effect. You may find that the question of "to bail or not to bail" is a time to exercise "tough love."

3. Drug and alcohol use. Although this could

be included in the negative, pre-arrest lifestyle of #2, there are two reasons why it needs to be in its own category: (1) its frequent presence behind many crimes and (2) the inability of many severe addicts to break their own addictions.

As a prison chaplain, I have taken to asking new inmates who come in with drug and alcohol addictions if they had recently (just prior to arrest) called out to God for help. The vast majority of them admit that they had. Is it, then, such a great leap of faith to consider that God knew that the only way they could gain freedom from addiction was to experience the imprisonment of their bodies? Of those asked, each one admitted to me that nothing else would have worked.

Sometimes, when inmates observe the deteriorating effect that substance abuse has had on their returning colleagues, they will say to one another, "Man, you weren't arrested—you were rescued!" This is why the presence of drug or alcohol use is a major factor when deciding whether or not to bail someone out of jail. If they are indeed addicted, then bailing him out returns him to drugs and alcohol before he has experienced the "natural detox" that incarceration provides. It also removes the consequences that may prevent a future disaster. Unabated drug and alcohol abuse can lead to something far worse than imprisonment. As in the case of the negative lifestyle, we ourselves can, in some cases, become enablers if we attempt to bail addicted persons out of jail too soon. This is especially true if this is not your loved one's first incarceration linked to substance abuse.

4. The emotional and mental state of the accused. This factor is important for first-time offenders. As someone who is close to the accused, you may know something about your loved one's emotional and psychological makeup that few others do. The law is not concerned with one's ability to handle a first incarceration; it is concerned only with arresting the violators of it. You and others close to the accused may be aware of a unique personality issue or condition that has a bearing on his inability to withstand a trip to jail.

5. Medical problems. If incarceration interferes with required medications that the offender must have, then this, too, is a factor to consider. Jails do provide medical assistance for common conditions; however, getting medication in a timely manner does not always happen. Also, if the medication required is expensive, do not be surprised to see the state—and especially the county—not respond too quickly. Interrupted medications are, unfortunately, a part of the consequences of the jail culture.

6. A young age. If the arrested individual is under seventeen or eighteen, most correctional facilities will separate the teen from his adult peers. But it is, nonetheless, a valid concern for friends and family. Some inmates who are over eighteen look much younger than they actually are. This creates a similar concern for their safety. Again, correctional administrations try to place these individuals in a safer environment than the general population (GP).

7. Weak in personal temperament or emotional makeup. If the incarcerated individual projects an affect that can be construed as very weak (physically or emotionally), then this, too, should be weighed when considering bail. The institution will tend to put such individuals in a more protective holding unit, but the behavior must usually be quite noticeable for them to do so.

8. First-time offenders. If the individual has not been a consistent behavior problem prior to his arrest, you may want to favorably consider bail. For some people (who are basically responsible but went temporarily off track), just the traumatic experience of being arrested and jailed is sufficient for them to get the point. Ask yourself if the situation was caused by an isolated bad choice that is unlikely to repeat, or whether it was the inevitable outcome of a repetitive pattern of misbehavior. Generally speaking, lifestyles of negativity, gross irresponsibility, criminal behavior and/or addiction usually warrant consequences.

And while any crime warrants consequences, there are bad choices that one can occasionally make that are still not considered significant trends in the life of the accused.

9. Relationship to the accused. What is your relationship to the person in jail? Spouse? Parent? Relative? Friend? Significant other? Each of these relationships has a different dynamic (and responsibility) attached to it.

a. Spouse. A wife, for example, must now face

financial pressures on the outside that a parent may not need to address as urgently. While parents may have to consider the expense of hiring an attorney, that tends to be the extent of their financial pressure. This is not true for a wife whose husband is now incarcerated.

If the husband had formerly contributed to the family expenses, she must now consider how to make it without that assistance. If she must relocate to less expensive living quarters, how will this affect her former routine? Not only does she have the hassle of packing and moving, she may now have to consider taking her children out of the school they were attending. What impact will this have on them? What about her job? Does she have one or must she now get one? If so, this will mean finding a trusted babysitter. These decisions are only the beginning of the major upheavals she will face. Financial pressure due to incarceration is more difficult, by far, on the surviving spouse (and children, if any) than on other relationships. Without support from sincere friends and family, many marriages disintegrate within the first year of incarceration.

b. Son or daughter. If the person in jail is a son or daughter who had been living at home, what is the current situation in the family? Who else will this incarceration affect? If it is a single-parent home, the incarcerated individual cannot expect the same measure of visitation or financial help that two parents could have provided. Are there other siblings? If so, how will this affect them?

As previously mentioned, the incarceration of

a child has driven many parents apart. The decision about bail is a case in point. Stereotypically, dads tend to err on the side of "justice" ("Let him sit there for a while!") and moms tend to err on the side of "mercy" ("Oh! We must get the dear child out of there!"). Great effort is needed to respect one another's perspectives. There must be a commitment to come together to make the wisest choice.

Another discovery some may experience is that things at home become less tense now that the troubled family member is absent. Many parents have felt somewhat guilty about admitting this, but they have discovered that the remaining members of the family unit are enjoying a relative time of peace and harmony now that the source of the tension is out of the house. This is especially true if the former lifestyle of the offending member was such that things at home were always in turmoil because of his behavior.

Be aware, also, of another dynamic that can affect the remaining members of the family. Because so much time and emotional energy are now focused on the incarcerated family member, the remaining children can sometimes feel overlooked or taken for granted. The truth is, more time is now needed with them. Not only are they missing their sibling and injecting their own emotions into the family grief, they can also feel neglected by comparison. This is sometimes referred to as the "Invisible, Good Child Syndrome."

This dynamic is usually unintended by the

parents. The other children could be well-behaved and be getting straight As at school; however, since all the attention of the family is now on the sibling in jail, the remaining children can experience feelings of emotional exclusion and eventual anger. As a result, they may also be dealing with a sense of guilt because they know they are angry with the one everyone else is so concerned about. The black sheep of the family is now robbing them of the attention they feel they need and deserve. Parents should be careful to make a concentrated effort to compensate for the emotional imbalance created by the incarcerated sibling.

c. Father or mother. If the offender in jail happens to be one of the parents, or primary caretakers of the home, this will have a severe impact on the little ones. Many children have been forced into foster homes because of the absence of their provider. And many more will likely end up being cared for by relatives who may or may not be pleased with this sudden arrangement, causing further strain on everyone involved. In most cases, emotionally torn grandparents are the usual recipients of such children.

If the role of the incarcerated parent has normally been a positive influence on the children, it may be wise to bail him out for the sake of family stability. However, the opposite may be true if the former activity of the incarcerated individual had been contributing to a harmful or negative environment in the home.

Increasingly, it is common to see both parents

and children serving time together. I recently met a woman whose mother was in jail with her. The woman was pregnant with the third generation, and the father of the child was on the men's side of the jail.

d. Girlfriend or boyfriend. If the accused is unmarried but was in a serious relationship with someone when arrested, he is often consumed (sometimes obsessed) with thoughts about how this will affect their continuing relationship. Generally speaking, the less trust, the more fear. If the person on the outside does not foresee hanging in there for the long haul, she should make this clear to the person in jail as soon as possible. While painful, it helps the inmate to adjust more quickly to his situation. If neither is clear about the future of the relationship, it is common to wait until the case has gone to court and a sentence determined before making rash decisions. Be aware that the more serious the crime, the longer it may take for the case to come to trial. (We will identify the various legal options and terms later.)

Unless the accused has been sentenced to many years in prison, do not entertain thoughts of getting married while the other is incarcerated. Such an action, while often motivated by a desire to demonstrate loyalty (and create a sense of security), nearly always ends in divorce within the first one or two years after release. The reasons for this are twofold: (1) they are getting married for the wrong reason and (2) they are currently living in two different worlds and building the relationship upon two different foundations. The inmate is living in his world and the visitor is living in her world. The relationship will change dramatically upon release.

Try to allow the absence to test the depth and sincerity of the relationship. If it is built on genuine trust, it will survive. The time of separation can be used to get to know each other on a deeper level than the physical.

e. Couple living together. If the parties have been living together, the uncertainty of their present situation now forces them to make a decision. Many of these relationships disintegrate at this point, but others are more determined than ever to hold it together. Although they had deferred the idea of cementing the relationship through marriage when they were both on the outside, it is common to now hear them referring to themselves as each other's "fiancé."

A further complication is that many of these couples already have children together. What will become of them? Since the incarceration now affects the remaining caretaker's finances, this person is often forced to find another place to live. It is also possible that the Division of Youth Services could step in and remove the children if the living situation is deemed sufficiently unstable or threatening to their well-being. The person in jail may be the biological parent but, in many states, his right to custody is now in jeopardy if the couple is unmarried. Typically, it is best for the surviving caretaker to seek refuge at the home of a stable relative, but only if that living situation is a positive environment for the children. At any rate, this relationship bears serious scrutiny in discerning the best course of action for the future. From here on out, the couple must put their own needs behind the needs of the children.

f. Other visitors or friends. True friends will hang in there; others will disappear. There is a saying in prison that goes: "It only takes a trip to jail to find out who your real friends are." The important issue for the accused person to consider, however, (and perhaps for the family to think about as well), is what type of influence these friends have been in the recent past. A sudden trip to jail or prison is a good opportunity to think about the factors that brought a person there in the first place. We are all responsible for our choices. "The devil made me do it" might have been a funny line for the comedian Flip Wilson, but if we are guilty, we are responsible for getting ourselves locked up. As we consider what changes we might make to avoid this in the future, we must include an honest look at our friendships. "We choose our friends, not our families," goes the old saying. In other words, there is something about our relationships with our friends that reveals a lot about who we are. Simply put, we are attracted to others who share our values.

The extent of future involvement with any peer group is ultimately a decision only the incarcerated person can make. Family members can make suggestions but they will seldom succeed in separating their loved one from negative friendships unless the loved one is convinced of the need as well. If you observe that the visitors list of the incarcerated one is filled with associates who have reinforced a negative lifestyle, this is not a good sign for the future.

But anyone can bail someone out. If you are the friend of someone who is incarcerated, you too must ask the same questions a family member would ask. What will be the consequences of bailing out your friend? Will he change? Will he go back to drugs? What will be the consequences of leaving him inside?

You must also consider that the bailed individual will feel less bound to stick around for his court appearance than he would have been if a family member had bailed him out. You, therefore, could be stuck with the entire amount.

What Is Bail?

"Bail" is a monetary amount set by the courts to ensure that the defendant shows up at the next prescribed court appearance. If granted, the defendant will be allowed his freedom until that time. In severe cases (or if the court decides the defendant is a flight risk), bail is not permitted. In most felony cases, bail amounts are usually set in the thousands of dollars. In misdemeanor cases, or lower classed felonies, the judge may have the liberty of issuing smaller bail amounts based on predetermined rates for certain offenses.

Once bail has been set, the entire amount must be paid to the court in either cash or bond before the defendant can be released. The amount is held in escrow (temporarily placing the valued amount into the hands of the court) until the defendant shows up for the designated court appearance. When the defendant appears at the appointed hearing, the money is returned to the one who posted the bail, or it may simply be continued if further court dates are necessary. (Be aware that bail can either be reduced or expanded at any subsequent court appearance. A request for bail reduction must be made by the attorney at the next hearing.)

In the event that bail has been permitted but the amount cannot be immediately paid, the defendant will be returned to custody until the bail money can be posted. In most cases, anyone can pay the bail on behalf of the defendant.

What Is a Bail Bondsman?

A "bail bondsman" is a business person who earns his or her money by posting the entire amount of the bail on behalf of clients who are unable (or unwilling) to pay the higher sum set by the court. The bondsman will place the entire amount on escrow with the courts and normally charge the client ten percent of the total bail requested. In other words, if the bail was set at ten thousand dollars, the amount paid to the bondsman will be one thousand dollars. This money will not be returned to you and is the cost of doing business with the bondsman. The bondsman, however, will have all his money returned to him once the defendant appears at the next hearing.

Do not encourage your loved one to "jump bail" (that is, not show up); bail bondsmen do not take kindly to forfeiting the total amount of bail money they posted. Further, you should be aware that in an effort to minimize their risk, many bondsmen require you to place something of equivalent (or higher) value as collateral. If your loved one jumps bail, you will forfeit whatever it was you placed as collateral.

Personal Recognizance

If the circumstances are minimal, or flight seems highly unlikely to the judge, he or she may permit a defendant to be released without posting *any* bail. This is usually called being released on one's own "personal recognizance." That is, the person promises to show up at the next hearing and nothing more is required of him than his word.

County Assistance

Some states have bail assistance provided by the county governments themselves. Check with your lawyer or the county clerk's office to see if this aid is available in your state. In Pennsylvania, for example, some counties will make the inmate aware that they will provide the full amount of the bail if the defendant (or his family) can come up with ten percent of the total amount. The difference between this arrangement and the way a bail bondsman operates is that when the defendant shows up for trial, eighty percent of the ten percent paid by the family is returned to them. (A bail bondsman keeps the entire ten percent.)

CHAPTER THREE

Communicating with Your Loved One

A great frustration to those on the outside is the inability to adequately communicate with their incarcerated loved one after first hearing the news. All we can say is, "Welcome to the Department of Corrections!"

Jail is not your local college dorm room. You cannot just pick up the phone and contact someone whenever you feel like it. In fact, you cannot call them at all; they must call you. Nor can they call you whenever *they* want; use of the phone is only permitted at certain times prescribed by the jail. You will eventually learn at which times your loved one is able to call, and make plans to be available during those times.

You must pay for the phone call, whether it is collect or through some prepaid arrangement with the phone company and the jail. And (for some reason I have yet to satisfactorily understand) these phone calls will be exorbitantly above the average rates for similar calls. Be prepared to pay three to four times more than you would for a regular, outside phone call. This unfortunate reality places an unnecessary burden upon the families, but it is a reality you will probably face. If your situation is such that you do not want to be contacted by the person in jail, you can ask the phone company to place a block on your phone if it comes from that destination.

After the initial shock of incarceration has worn down a bit, you will adjust to the precious moments you are able to communicate with your loved one, whether it is by phone or by personal visit. (Our next booklet in the series will include suggestions for the visiting experience.) At the beginning, the air surrounding these early communications will be filled with a variety of heavy emotions; sorrow, shame, guilt or remorse may all weave their strands into the fabric of your loved one's conversation. Many inmates seek to comfort you during this time; they feel they have let you down and often feel badly about it.

But like the darker clouds that lurk within a stormy sky, do not be surprised to discover that other, less friendly emotions may begin to appear over time. Anger, blame, bitterness, impatience, manipulation and ingratitude are among the chief ones to which you should be alert. Any of these expressions can appear occasionally; it is quite normal, given the circumstances. But what you should be watching out for is if these negative "clouds" become the predominant attitude whenever you meet or speak with each other.

The Dark Side

Newly arrested individuals often exhibit a tendency to exaggerate their negative surroundings when speaking to you. After your first few visits or phone calls from the jail, you may notice that your loved one is in a constant state of negative agitation. Some of this is quite normal; jail is no fun. But some residents pour out such a consistently negative description of their situation and surroundings that their mood is always sour and bitter. Some will try to put undue pressure on you through these negative vibes, hoping to emotionally manipulate or threaten you into bailing them out. You should resist this—for both your sakes.

Others can sound extremely frightened, vulnerable and unprotected. You may think this is obvious (given the fact that they are newly locked up with strangers who have been charged with criminal behavior), but what I am describing here is the expression of an exaggerated state of fearful realities. In other words, what they are telling you is often not exactly the way it is. There are six, very good possibilities for why they do this.

1. They want out. Whether guilty or innocent, your loved one does not want to be in jail a second longer than is necessary. You are his loved one on the outside. To him, that means you can (he hopes) change his current status by getting him out. "Do something!" is the real cry being issued from the heart. Very likely, he is afraid—especially if this is his first incarceration. By pouring out his fears to you in the most convincing manner possible, he hopes to convey his sense of urgency.

It would be wise, however, to consider that the urgency of the report carries the emotional spin of fear. For example, I have often been surprised to learn that a loved one has told his parents (or outside people) about conditions at the jail that did not actually exist. Or, if there were some element of truth to the account, it varied greatly in terms of actual degree.

2. It gets the focus off of them. A second reason for these frightful reports is that by making complaints about the jail, its staff or policies, the absence of amenities or even other inmates who have threatened him, he succeeds in diverting your attention from the actions that got him there in the first place. This behavior is especially effective if you are prone to make excuses for him; you will find yourself quickly becoming angry at those "other" threats he is describing and view your loved one as a victim.

3. Manipulation. By painting a terrible picture of the situation, the individual may succeed in maneuvering you into taking the steps he wants you most to take. (Which is, more than likely, to bail him out.) This may be a conscious manipulation on his part, or an unconscious one, but it is still manipulation. If you have been given to making excuses for the individual in the past, be careful that you are not further enabling him by giving in to his emotional manipulation.

4. It *seems* that bad. Your loved one's perception of the nightmare into which he suddenly finds himself plunged may greatly influence the way he describes it to you. This is especially true if it is the first incarceration. However, his description may be coming from an initial perception that is, as yet, unable to distill fact from fiction, or fear from reality. If this is, in fact, the reason, his alarm should decrease as time passes. As he adjusts to his environment, you should notice an easing of his tension.

It is also possible that other inmates may have over-dramatized the common fears and stereotypes about jail just to scare him or tease him because he is new. After all, how would he know?

5. Even big kids need their mommies. Sometimes, underneath it all, there is still an unconscious desire to "show mommy the boo-boo." The one in jail would never admit to this, of course, but behind some of the reports of how bad everything is, there can still be the old dynamic of telling mom (or dad) how much it hurts.

6. Acceptance. Do not forget that the person is having his first contact with you after allegedly messing up. There is likely to be a bit of uncertainty as to how you will receive him. He expects that you may be mad or disappointed, but he still wants to know that his basic relationship with you is secure. As in #2, by diverting your attention to the negative environment, he may succeed in appealing to your "merciful" side, as opposed to your "judgment" side.

Of the six reasons we have listed for why some inmates will exaggerate the awfulness of their situation, we can certainly sympathize with the last three.

Hearing These Fearful Reports

Most family members tend to panic and fear the worst when receiving the news that their loved one has been arrested and detained. This is not only typical; it is understandable. But when hearing a fearful report from their loved one further compounds the situation, it only adds fuel to the fire. Perceptions (by both of you) can vary wildly at initial stages. So what should you do when you receive a terrifying report from your loved one?

First, listen to him and genuinely sympathize with him. You do not need to express any skepticism regarding the description of his experience; it may, after all, be true. What he most needs is the verbal comfort of his family (or spouse, or loved one). But try to place the basic nature of his complaint into one of two categories: (1) *must* take action or (2) *must not* take action. For example, is he describing uncomfortable jail realities such as overcrowding, taunts or bad food (category two), or is he describing the real threat of physical abuse (category one)?

If what he is telling you has information that contains the genuine threat of physical injury, call the institution immediately. Document the time and date of your phone call. The physical threat may include the interruption of treatment for a serious, ongoing medical condition, or it may be in the form of a physical threat by another inmate. Most correctional facilities try their best to protect the safety of their inmates, but there can always exist situations of which they are unaware. A phone call to the jail's administrator or person in charge lets the institution know that *you* know of a possible threat to your loved one. Before doing this, however, you should always ask your loved one if he *wants* you to make the phone call. Do not make this decision unilaterally. A call from the outside alerting the jail administration of a potential threat to your loved one may force the correctional staff to place him in a special part of the jail that is designed to protect inmates from other inmates. Usually called Protective Custody (PC), this area is looked upon with disdain by the inmates in the regular population. (PC is where most sexual offenders or informers are held.) Once one is branded a "PC inmate," it now becomes unsafe for that person to ever return to the GP at a later time. However, "taking a PC" is a wise decision for those who are in a genuinely threatened situation.

If the nature of the perceived danger is due to an urgent medical need, you must be sure it is serious. Most county jails are not set up to provide advanced medical treatment due to financial restraints and the high turnover of inmates. Until an inmate has actually been sentenced, there is even less of an incentive to provide for anything beyond basic medical care. But if you feel the situation simply cannot go unattended, these facilities do have infirmaries with medical staff in attendance. For more serious medical emergencies, arrangements will be made to send the resident to a nearby hospital under correctional oversight and security.

In summary, if the nature of the negative information you are receiving from your loved one concerns the living conditions or other uncomfortable realities normally associated with being in jail, you may sympathize with him, but do not call the institution or go to battle with the administration over such things. You will seldom succeed in changing the situation and you may even draw unnecessary (and unfavorable) attention toward your loved one. But in the final analysis, if you deem the threat to be of a genuine and serious nature, then by all means contact the chief administrator of the institution.

CHAPTER FOUR

The Legal Process

It is not our purpose to provide a lengthy discussion on the entire legal process; that would be beyond the scope of this booklet. However, following are some common things for you to consider as you go forward.

The Charges

What is the accused being charged with? How serious is it? Is it a misdemeanor or a felony? Misdemeanors are lesser crimes that usually carry only a fine or probation as a sentencing consequence. Felonies are serious crimes that usually carry jail or prison sentences and are divided into categories ranging from most severe to less severe. (For example, Class A felonies are more severe than Class D felonies.)

Remember that the charges cited at the time of the arrest may later be changed or modified before the actual trial. Arresting officers write the charges as they have observed them; but court proceedings may alter the actual charges based on evidentiary hearings. That means that the evidence to support the original charges may or may not be substantial enough to support them in a legal confrontation.

An arrest is not a conviction. It is important from a legal standpoint (as well as a relational one) to remember that although your loved one has been charged with a crime, he has not yet been found guilty in a court of law. We are still a nation that works on the principle that one is innocent until proven guilty. However, you will soon discover that while this is true in legal principle, the whole process seems otherwise. It *feels* like everyone you meet in the process already thinks you are guilty, just by virtue of being *in* the system.

Still, no one can be sentenced until an appropriate court has legally determined guilt. "Due process" is still defined as being "a constitutional provision guaranteeing an accused person a fair and impartial trial." However, what is more important for us to consider here is that one can also remain in custody up to (and throughout) his entire court proceedings. Depending on the case and the severity of the charges, this can sometimes be years. If one cannot afford bail, or if bail has been refused, a defendant must remain incarcerated until the outcome of the legal proceedings is over.

Understanding what happens next. Let us say your loved one has been arrested and is in the local county jail or city lockup. You cannot get him out until he has appeared before a judge for an arraignment hearing. This may be the very next morning or, if it is a weekend, not until the following Monday or Tuesday.

A city jail (as opposed to a county jail) is a temporary lockup and is used only because that is the city (or local precinct) out of which the arresting officers operate, and in which the alleged offense took place. If the city is a major metropolitan area, then the defendants will most likely be moved to larger holding facilities operated by the city.

In the early stages of the process, it is important to remind your loved one that he should not volunteer any comments to the police regarding the case without his lawyer present. Anything he verbally volunteers can be later used against him if the events ultimately lead to a trial.

The Arraignment

The next step is the arraignment. The arraignment is not a trial. As such, it will not be the time for the person to argue the merits of his case. It is merely a proceeding that officially enters him into the criminal justice system and determines how his case will proceed from there. However, if it is for a fairly minor offense (and only if he wishes to plead guilty) the judge can decide, then and there, what the consequences will be.

The release of your loved one is usually not possible until he has been arraigned. In most cases, arraignments must take place within two or three working days of an arrest, depending upon your state's laws. The following steps take place at an arraignment:

If the courtroom is not in the same building as the jail, your loved one will be transported by security van to the courthouse. He will appear in a courtroom (usually crowded with many others who are facing arraignments) and wait for his name and case to be called. If you are a family member, come prepared to sit there for hours; this is typical. However, if your loved one is in police custody, most courts will hear those cases first.

Be prepared to see your loved one file into the courtroom in handcuffs and leg shackles. This is a sight that many parents and loved ones have been emotionally unprepared to see. However, this is normal procedure for anyone being transported in police custody. The police are concerned only with providing the security of the transport; it is not their assignment to determine guilt or innocence. Your loved one will usually enter the courtroom in a single file with other defendants who have also been in custody. They will be made to sit in a special, protective area. You may sit as close to that area as you are allowed to, but you will not be allowed to sit with your loved one.

When the case is called, the charges will be read and the judge will ask the defendant two questions: (1) if he understands the charges against him and (2) how he wishes to plead to the charges. If an attorney has been retained, he or she will usually speak on the prisoner's behalf at this time. If your loved one does not have an attorney and does not wish to plead until he has legal representation, the judge will enter a "not guilty" plea and advise him of his right to a public defender (if he cannot afford one). At that time, the judge will set a date for his next court appearance. The judge will also notify him of any possible bail arrangement that, if paid, could enable him to stay out of jail until the next court date.

Plea Responses

When the judge or magistrate asks your loved one how he pleads to the charges, the courts generally accept only one of three responses: "not guilty," "guilty" or "no contest." If he (or the lawyer on his behalf) pleads "not guilty," the judge will consult the official court calendar and assign him the date and time of his next court appearance. Nothing else will happen at the arraignment other than the setting of a bail amount.

If your loved one feels the charges are warranted, and if they are of a fairly minor nature (such as a misdemeanor), two other pleas are also available: "guilty" or "no contest." (A "no contest" plea is also known as pleading "nolo" or "nolo contendere." This literally means, "I do not wish to contend it.") By pleading "nolo," your loved one is neither admitting guilt nor denying it, but he agrees to accept whatever the court decides as a punishment.

If he chooses to plead "guilty," he is legally agreeing with the charges made against him and will accept whatever sentence the court may lawfully administer.

At crowded arraignment hearings, judges do not generally want to hear arguments for your loved one's defense; they simply want to know how he pleads and, once entered, will either set a future court date or accept his plea of guilty.

Plea Bargains

A plea bargain is an arrangement between the prosecution and the defense in which both parties agree to accept a predetermined punishment in return for an admission of guilt. Basically, the state is saying, "If you will save us the expense of a trial, we will spare you the extra degree of punishment that we will probably succeed in convicting you of."

Plea bargains are scary. It is one thing to watch them on a television show; it is an entirely different thing to face this decision yourself. In the end, they are a gamble. If your loved one believes he is innocent, or that the charges against him are unsupportable, he may want to continue with a trial by jury. On the other hand, if he feels that the offer made by the prosecutor is acceptable (or that he can tolerate it), he may want to accept the plea bargain. Many defendants usually wind up somewhere in the middle, not knowing exactly which way to turn.

In some circumstances, the person may be faced with realizing that the charges are not exactly accurate but that a conviction is still possible. Only you and your loved one can make the decision that is ultimately acceptable for both of you. But try not to second-guess yourself later. You can only make the best decision you can, based on the facts that were at your disposal at the time.

It is definitely a time for prayer.

CHAPTER FIVE

Hiring an Attorney

Hiring a lawyer is one of the most important decisions you will make throughout this entire process. A good lawyer is worth it; but a disinterested (or mediocre, or unscrupulous) lawyer will leave you extremely discouraged—and quite a bit poorer. Unfortunately, in terms of adequate defense, our legal system is not created equal for all of us. Expensive, experienced lawyers tend to do better for their clients than lesser-experienced ones. While it is true that even rich people go to jail, it is also true that they do not go as often—or for as long. But it will not do you (or your loved one) any good moaning over the inequalities of our justice system. You must still make a decision. Here are nine realities to consider when deciding upon a lawyer:

1. How to find one. If you have ever visited the Yellow Pages and looked under "lawyers" or "attorneys," the blatant advertisements seem to go on forever. Some law offices operate with a high standard of professionalism; some do not. How do you know which is which and whom to choose? The ideal situation is to have either a trusted friend as an able attorney or someone who has done reliable work for you in the past. Lacking this, your next best bet is the personal recommendation of someone who has been a satisfied recipient of an attorney's services and can vouch for his or her abilities.

Today, you also have the advantage of using the Internet. You could search for sites (or blogs) that supply comments on various law firms and/or the personal experiences others have had with specific attorneys. There are also websites that supply general information on where to find law firms that specialize in certain types of cases and in which states they operate (http://www.lawyers.findlaw.com and http://www.martindale.com are two).

To some degree, your optimum confidence level in any attorney will be rooted in the level of personal comfort and trust you have in him or her, or on the testimony of reliable, former recipients of his or her services. This is a highly charged emotional time for you. For this reason, it is necessary that you do your homework when choosing a lawyer. Find someone who will be realistic with you about all the eventual expenses that may be incurred. Also, find someone you can relate to on a personal level. Your level of personal trust is going to be a major factor in how you feel *after* this is all over.

2. Expense. Whoever you wind up choosing, one thing is fairly certain—it is not going to be cheap. If you hire a lawyer, be prepared to spend a good deal of money for which you had not likely budgeted. Very few families or friends were saving money for the sudden incarceration of a loved one. If your savings account is not very deep, this experience could very easily empty it. Be prepared to seriously consider your options.

If it is a fairly serious case, you must also be prepared to spend significantly more money than your attorney originally told you it would cost. Do your best to get as tight an estimate as you can from your attorney before hiring him or her. Get it in writing. Some attorneys have asked for substantially more than their original estimate, once the trial has begun. You may think this is unfair, but it is quite common. Even when told by their lawyers that the original estimate would be close to the total cost, defendants and their families have been shocked to be later told that in order for the firm to continue handling their case, they would need substantially more money. When a family objects and tries to remind the attorney of the original agreement, the lawyer responds (usually in "legalese") with an answer that justifies the surprise price hike. He or she may say that the case took an "unexpected turn" and that it has required more expense than he or she had originally thought. He or she may remind you that you had agreed to an hourly expense and that it was now requiring more hours of his or her time (and, of course, that of his or her staff's). He or she may want to hire "expert witnesses" or charge you for expenses, errands, filings or motions that "were necessary" in order to give your loved one "the best chance of winning." We, as non-lawyers, most likely do not know what papers need filing or which motions must be made. In the end, you are forced to either terminate his or her services (and lose any money you may have already paid him or her) or pay the extra money

You do have legal recourse, however. If you feel you have been deceived or cheated by an attorney, call the office of your state's Attorney General and report the situation to him or her. All attorneys are under the jurisdiction and oversight of the state's legal commission and any practitioner can lose his or her license to practice if convicted of unethical behavior. Do not hesitate to make this phone call if you feel you have been treated fraudulently.

(See http://www.naag.org/ag/full_ag_table.php for a complete listing of all state Attorneys General and their contact information.)

3. No lawyer can guarantee the outcome of any trial. While hiring a good lawyer can increase your odds of winning, or succeed in getting a more desirable outcome, no one can guarantee the outcome of any trial.

In the end, what you want to say about your attorney is that he or she tried his or her best. Win or lose, if you feel your attorney took a personal interest in your case and supplied sufficient effort, it will go a long way in helping you come to grips with the outcome. There are good lawyers, mediocre lawyers and bad lawyers; do your homework. Ask for help from friends or trusted contacts that have hired attorneys; get their input. References and recommendations can be helpful, but remember that the outcome achieved by an attorney in one case does not guarantee the same outcome in another. Every case is different.

4. Should we hire a lawyer or go with a court-appointed one? Many people feel that because they are getting a public defender (also known as a "court-appointed lawyer"), they will not be getting a good defense. This is not true; sometimes you can get a very good court-appointed lawyer. Public defenders are full-fledged attorneys who are either part of a public defense pool, or may be part of a rotation in which local lawyers give a certain amount of *pro bono* (donated) time. Others offer their services for the experience they will gain.

However, it is also generally accepted that the incentive for such individuals to "go the extra mile" for you is not great. Human nature would dictate that few people would be inclined to spend a lot of their own time and expense on a *pro bono* case when they are also handling cases for which they are being privately retained. Ask yourself this question: If court-appointed lawyers are working on cases for which they are being minimally paid, and also working on cases for which they are being privately retained, which cases will likely get the most attention and effort?

5. A public defender is free to the defendant. While you may have some reservations about the performance and effort of your court-appointed lawyer, remember that you are receiving his or her services for free. If you choose to go this route, resist the temptation to second-guess yourself later.

6. A public defender is primarily for those

who cannot afford an attorney. Many people who could well afford to hire an attorney think that a court-appointed lawyer is their natural right. While this is a common perception, and seldom challenged by the courts for fear of violating a civil right, it was originally intended as a service to those who genuinely could not afford one. The service is in place to ensure that each citizen's constitutional rights will not be violated. This right is there to protect you. If you can't afford a lawyer, the system will provide one for you. And for many defendants, the decision to hire an attorney is not within their means.

7. Do not doubt in the dark what you knew to be true in the light. Christians often use this statement to encourage themselves in hard times. They remind themselves of the promises of God that they knew to be true before a difficult situation befell them. Then they remind themselves that the promises are still true—although they are more difficult to see.

Whether or not you are a Christian, you can still use the same principle. For example, if you decide (based on the facts that you had at the time) that your wisest course of action is to go with a court-appointed lawyer, then no matter how it later turns out, do not beat yourself up if everything does not go as you had hoped. You made the best decision you could, based on the facts that you had at the time. It will not help you or your loved one if you wind up living in the barren lands of "If-only" or "What-if." Do not forget that even those who have hired the best attorneys money can buy are not guaranteed the outcomes for which they had hoped.

8. Defendants can ask for another court-appointed lawyer. Many people think they are stuck with whomever they are given as a public defender. If you are doubtful or unhappy about the services of your court-appointed lawyer, the defendant still has the right to request that another attorney be provided for him in order to meet the expectation of being adequately defended. This does not mean that the presiding judge will always go along with the request, but you are entitled to make it.

The dark side of the decision to switch, however, is that such a move will delay the proceedings of the trial. A new lawyer will have to receive everything from the previous lawyer and be brought up to speed on the proceedings thus far. And who is to say what level of satisfaction the new appointee will bring? Additionally, if the accused is not out on bail, this usually means spending more time in jail before sentencing. And even if the accused is out on bail, it means that life cannot return to normal until everything is over. Prolonging the trial may also have an impact on other life-factors such as finances, employment, family relationships and relocation.

9. Probability of conviction. A final category to consider when hiring an attorney is the likelihood of conviction. If the evidence or witnesses against the defendant is such that a conviction is extremely likely, then it may still be in your best interest to hire a good lawyer. Depending on the range of punishment possibilities for the crime, a sharp defense lawyer's best contribution to you may be to lessen the severity of the sentence.

CHAPTER SIX

God's Plan for You

The first five sections of this booklet supplied various components of the incarceration process that we felt were important facts for you to consider. Now I would invite you to ask yourself this question: Have you at any time throughout this journey wondered if God could have had a purpose in it for you? If your answer is yes, then please read on.

God wants to use this trying experience to lead you to the most important truth of all—that there is a God, that He is a good God, and that He seeks to reward those who diligently seek Him.[3] Sometimes we must reach our lowest depths before we look upward. God knows what it takes to get our attention. Recall again how some inmates greet their friends who are returning to jail by saying, "Man, you weren't arrested—you were rescued!" It is clear to them that their friends had been on a headlong spiral to something far worse than jail—perhaps even death.

In thirty years of prison ministry, I have met countless individuals who have admitted that if

---

3. Hebrews 11:6

God had not arranged the consequences of their actions to result in the severe mercy of incarceration, they were heading for sure destruction. So God stopped them. He did for them what they were unable to do for themselves.

There are things far worse than going to jail. Many inmates will tell you that they believe their jail experience is hell. But this is only true on the physical level; there is a spiritual hell as well. And unless we receive God's forgiveness for our sins while we are in *this* world, we shall not experience it in the next.

Many people think that if their "good" deeds outweigh their "bad" ones, then the Judge will be lenient with them. But the Bible does not use such language. A person is either perfectly sinless in every way, or guilty. There is no in-between.

You and I were created to know God and to enjoy Him forever; that was God's intention from the beginning. But the Bible clearly states that all of us are lawbreakers. *Everyone* has sinned and fallen short of God's glory and perfection.[4] And all of us will face the ultimate Judge someday. The Bible says that after we die we will all appear before the judgment seat of Christ and have to give an account for the things we did during our lifetimes.[5] There are no plea bargains with God, no probation, no parole and no such thing as a "not guilty" plea. The right consequence for our sins against God is an eternal punishment in hell,

---

4. Romans 3:23
5. 2 Corinthians 5:10

separated from His presence forever.[6]

Many people think that breaking God's law is like breaking a single windowpane in a window that has many panes. As long as most of the panes are not broken, they reason that God will overlook the broken ones. But God's law is not a window with a lot of compartmental panes; it is more like a single, plate glass window. You cannot break just part of it without breaking it all. This is also why many people on the outside think that your jailed loved one is worse than they are. They think your loved one has broken more windowpanes because he is in jail; therefore, they believe God will accept them because they are "better." This is not true. Jesus said it is the sick who know they need a doctor.[7] This is why so many who find themselves in jail or prison come to Christ for the forgiveness of their sins. They know they need a doctor.

Did you ever stop to think that a person in jail, who *knows* he needs God's forgiveness, is spiritually better off than someone on the outside who does not? It may seem strange to think so, but according to Jesus' own words, it is true. This is why Jesus said to the self-righteous people of His day: "I tell you the truth, the tax collectors and the prostitutes are entering the Kingdom of God ahead of you."[8] If it takes a trip to jail to finally slow us down long enough to listen to the words

---

6. Romans 6:23; 2 Thessalonians 1:9
7. Mark 2:17
8. Matthew 21:31

of God, then I say to you that it was all worth it. I myself served a prison sentence when I was a young man; I *know* this is true.

God knew we had all fallen short of *His* perfection; He also knew that without His level of perfection we would never see the Kingdom of God. So, like arresting an addict by sending him to jail, God did for us what we could not do for ourselves—He stepped out of heaven and *He* paid the sentence that *our* sins deserved.

Can you imagine a situation here on earth where a judge rightly sentences someone to jail for a crime for which he was guilty, and then, instead of sending the convicted person to jail, the judge gets up from the bench and turns himself into the jailers in place of the convicted person? The judge then goes to jail for the crimes of the guilty person, and the guilty person goes free. We will probably never see anything like that here on earth, but that is exactly what the God of heaven has done for you.

I have met many people in prison who are genuinely sorry for their crimes, but they do not get to go free simply because they are sorry. They must still pay the penalty for their actions.

But God sent His only Son, Jesus Christ, into the world to save guilty people like you and me. And to prove that this was all the work of God, Jesus rose victoriously from the dead three days after He was crucified! And all those who put their trust in Jesus will also rise from the dead.

Are you sorry for your sins? Do you want to experience God's forgiveness? Then know this for sure: when God had His only Son nailed to a cross, it was in payment for your sins. He took your place. Are you ready to change your mind about the way you have lived, and trust the testimony that God has given us about His Son, Jesus? Shall you not give Him the reward that His suffering for you has earned?

God has a plan for you as you deal with the incarceration of your loved one. He does not want you to simply suffer through it—He wants to come alongside you and transform your life in the midst of the unsettling waters. Please let Him. If you are ready to have Him transform your life forever, then let the following prayer be the sincere cry of your heart:

"Dear Father God, I am sorry for my sins. I am sorry for everything I have ever done that has been opposed to your good and perfect law. I admit that I have broken it many times and do not deserve to be in your presence. I am sincerely sorry and I truly desire to turn away from my sinful life. I now understand that you gave your only Son, Jesus Christ, to die on the cross as the full and only payment for my sins. I know that you gave Him as a gift to me—and I want to receive that gift. I believe in Jesus Christ and trust Him totally for the payment of all my sins. Although I know that I do not deserve it, I happily receive your forgiveness and love. In the name of Jesus I make this request, Amen."